PATCHWORK

✦

PATCHWORK

✦

Kuli Kohli

OFFA'S PRESS
2016

First published in 2016 by Offa's Press,
Ferndale, Pant, Oswestry, Shropshire, SY10 9QD.

Re-printed in 2018

ISBN: 978-0-9955225-1-0

Typeset in Baskerville Old Face
Designed by Marie Jones, printed and bound
by Lion FPG Limited,
Oldbury Road, West Bromwich, B70 9DQ.

CONTENTS

Patchwork

Countless experiences,
a myriad of thoughts,
memories, feelings,
complex yet simple.

Combined from rags,
various textures, fabrics,
rough, smooth cloth,
distinctly scented.

Tinted temperaments,
diverse arrangements,
shapes and designs
patterns of a broad life.

Tears of sorrow, regret,
tears of joy, pleasure,
displays a patchwork
compassionately made.

Coloured with sensations,
threaded with strength,
a needle, piece by piece,
devotion in every strand.

I'll keep collecting
these sentiments,
I'll keep sewing
endlessly, forever.

Handmade, homemade
prepared with love,
a complete collage of
my life uniquely crafted.

Scapegoat

For Jas

She would follow me all over the place
where mother and I dug up *mitti**, sowing.
Spinning broken bike wheels in open space,
balance crops upon our heads, sweat flowing.

Once she followed me all the way to school,
where she was not welcomed. I took lashes
on my hand and stood in the corner; a fool
in the scorching sun. I loathed *Masterji's* classes.

With twigs and bark, I'd greet her at the gate,
stroke, feed her away from my elder brother.
When I was away from home, she'd wait,
she'd linger like a kid waiting for her mother.

She'd give us thick milk morning and night.
When she fell ill, she'd yearn for me, crying.
I'd pat her patchy coat, she'll be alright,
little did I know she was in pain and dying.

One day I returned, my *bakri* wasn't there,
I searched the *pind*, our *zameen*, everywhere.
I came back. My heart sank. The aroma in the air.
My brother was cooking curry, not a trace of care.

mitti – soil (Punjabi)
Masterji – teacher (Punjabi)
bakri – goat (Punjabi)
pind – village (Punjabi)
zameen – land (Punjabi)

An Interpretation Of Wolverhampton

I heard a friend from Birmingham say,
"If yow thought Brummies sounded funny,
man, wait'll yow get ta Woolverramton, t'ay
y'naa, them am tekkin the piss an it aye!"
English? I believe it's an interpretation thing.

Once I met an old Indian woman at a bus stop,
"Bulbulhamtan noo jaandi hai bus?" she asked.
Smiling, I nodded, "Haanji, it's only a short hop."
Chuckling to myself, "My entertaining city, it's top!"
Punjabi? I believe it's an interpretation thing.

A Black-Caribbean man stopped and enquired,
"Ary yu dat 'umaan hoo work in di counceel?"
Confused, I asked him to repeat what he required,
"Hulvahaamtown Counceel, mi dear gal!" he fired.
Patois? I believe it's an interpretation thing.

Every category of human being all within reach,
A specially formulated city; a hint of prejudice.
Engaging everyday life; diverse tongues, speech,
An accidental evolution; an awareness to teach,
Wolverhampton? It's an interpretation thing.

The Rag Doll

To Fellow Rag Dolls Living With Cerebral Palsy

Silk, linen, velvet, cotton, wool;
Made from all sorts; textures, fabrics,
Buttons, ribbons, hips made from zips,
Whoops-a-daisy and falling to bits.

Her heart is made of golden fluff,
Her smile is stitched shining bright,
Now and again she's not there, quite,
Her spirit shines like ultra violet light.

Droops, dangles her limbs and neck,
Durable to all types of wear and tear,
Broken, damaged here and there,
People stare; she just does not care.

Battling, juggling impossibilities,
Shining diamond sequined eyes,
Always ready to give you a surprise,
Like a cartoon, she'll always survive.

Has trouble with her physical being,
Words tangled in the laces of her head,
Still figuring out what you have just said,
Jerking, jolting to the day she's dead!

Clive Sahib

From childhood I desired fortune and fame to be forever mine,
I wanted class, status, prominence and the world to remember,
a significant man, 1st Baron Robert Clive; England's treasure.

An adolescent "good for nothing, a tearaway, a spoiled brat".
Young and feral like a Bengal tiger waiting to be let loose
out of a simple Shropshire village into the vast land of India.

I worked for the East India Company - like a prison sentence,
depression overtook me; I drank potions of hate and rage,
then joined the army. I rose rapidly and lucratively to the top.

From a clerk to a conqueror, the Empire belonged to me,
pride and victory for England, I focused on power and politics;
I showed them what I was all about. I was the British Raj.

I laughed at natives, their funny looking gods and goddesses,
I had power and position, born to a category of superior race,
seized with cannons, heartless strengths, a craze to snatch it all.

India was a goldmine; I wasn't letting it slip into any other hands,
I fought off the French, the Dutch or anyone who got in the way.
I bribed, looted and killed the Indians, the foolish, inferior natives.

Maharajas, lands, sandhi, treaties, lagaan*, very easily bought.
I grabbed riches, took them back to Shropshire to live like a king;
my family and friends turned on me; my wealth was the problem.

I have everything, yet nothing at all; life isn't as splendid;
unsatisfied, broken, the end has come; opium, a knife, a gun.
I have been defeated by life; a memory of pride and greed.

*Maharajas - any of various Indian princes - any of the rulers
of the former native states. Sandhi - a binding agreement / treaty
(Punjabi). Lagaan - taxes (Hindi).

Papaji's Curry Garden

In our oblong garden there is a lawn
bordered with trees, shrubs, flowers,
roses and vegetables nicely drawn,
our Papaji's labour measured in hours.

The vampires flee, scared off by the garlic,
being chased away by the runner beans,
onions, coriander, fenugreek; so aromatic,
plants dotted about; tiny pods of chickpeas.

Applemint and peppermint everywhere,
green leafy spinach and firm mustard,
white flowered radish pods waving in the air,
burgundy rhubarb; so tasty with custard.

Pumpkins' vigorous vines sprawl and creep,
streaked courgettes' golden flowers gleam,
his passion shows when he digs soil deep,
Papaji is lost in his world of earthly dream.

Doesn't have knowledge of the flowers' names,
he calls them by character, colour, shapes,
"Laal, peela, neela, hara,"* Punjabi fun'n'games,
nurtured, enveloping mesh. Nothing escapes.

But the kids want to play football and cricket,
furious Papaji bellows his often repeated call
to the birds, fat pigeons, kids running for a wicket:
"My plants! Don't kill them or I'll kill you all!"

*Red, yellow, blue, green (Punjabi)

Collecting Gems

A childhood full of memories close to nature.
I remember my first school; special and striking,
majestic gardens, woods crammed with creatures,
owls, lawns, hollies, great conifers, rhododendrons.

My attention lay among the green undergrowth;
nettles, reeds, marsh flowers and veined thorns,
in a ditch over a small stone moss-carpeted wall,
a little pond of tadpoles; speckled frogs on logs.

My favourite was the top lawn near the woods,
where the summer scents fed all my senses,
an earthy smell of wood, leaves, soil, vegetation,
dew drizzled roses and freshly mowed lawns.

Impatiently waiting for the bells to sing, "Play time!"
I would rush out blindly into the sparkling sunlight,
making my way up the stony stairs, on all fours,
to the row of horse chestnut and sycamore trees.

Up the bank, flat on my back on the shaded green,
gazing into the sky watching the chandelier flowers;
emerald stars waving at me through wispy breeze,
waiting for the ruddy diamond conkers to plunge.

The teacher told me it was too early, I did not believe.
I would wait every day for the conkers to drop down.
Then, finally, after the summer, the freshness decays;
rusty tints. I'd eagerly gather tarnished seeds like gems.

The Drop

Near the drop of a cliff, my heart fails,
my body refuses to move, I freeze:
'Why did I follow these narrow trails?'
Caught between the land, sea and breeze.

He gently hauls me up, tells me to focus,
step by step, holds tight on to my hand,
"You can do it, it's not all hocus-pocus."
I sense his worry, it's not as he planned.

Constantly staring down at my shoes,
wearing blinkers; a tunnel vision in force.
My wit backing me along the path I choose,
amid the scent of coconut, vanilla gorse.

"I'd put you in my rucksack, carry you,"
We laugh about my palsy, passing through.

The Brown Girl In The Rain

Through the twisting zigzag country lanes,
wet sprays from the speedy vehicles;
the rain beats down onto the metronomic
sweep of the windscreen wipers; the calming
music on the radio carries her far, far away,
where she thinks she is without restraints.

In the moist valleys, the breathtaking views,
she is captured by the streams of running water,
the spongy wet kisses of falling soft rain upon her lips.
Carpeted below her feet, a pattern of soggy,
fire coloured leaves, berries, fungus, slippery mud,
and slews around, juddering in the slimy sludge.

Dying ferns like rust on the ancient layers of earth,
that only doggedness can endure. The auburn hills
beam at the unsteady brown girl, welcoming her
to the edge of life - where erratically she's in charge,
yet the fear of her falling and failing her mission
often enters her mind, still, she holds her position.

Discarded

Father, you told me,
"This daughter of mine
will be lost without me
and be left far behind."

Your exact words were,
"Without me, you're nothing,
if you leave now, you won't
manage to achieve a thing;

take a close look at yourself:
walking, talking you dread,
yet you dream of a full life,
but can't even afford bread!"

Discarded, your poor princess.
Father, you were so wrong.
My shadow listened, placed
telling words into my song.

Resilient

In every way possible
she knocked me down.
I was her supple rag doll -
I did not cry nor frown.

Twisted, crumpled and scolded,
dragged about, in and out.
I choked in silence, I was folded
seamless, flawed and ragged.

No sign of core damage. I was robust,
if I had been made of porcelain
she would have turned me to dust.

Stubborn Roots

In Memory of Jyoti Singh

A land where gods and goddesses are said to have walked?
It's time to wake up and pull up these stubborn roots.

Incredible India claims to be transforming fast...
yet has it become a molesting monster?

Was there ever a time when girls and women could be safe
on the streets, in villages, cities, taxis, buses, trains alone?

Maaji said, "Stay away from prying, lustful men's eyes,
they are like predators searching to attack pretty looking prey."

She is psychologically, physically and verbally abused if her
dowry isn't up to standard or she doesn't give birth to a son.

Accepted by a culture and proud of female infanticide,
honour killings, burned alive by the women themselves.

"Oh dear, there's been another accidental death," they said.
"Only a woman," the police are unable to help or investigate.

Ruined, raped, silenced and forced to accept it's her mistake,
leading to shame, dishonour and eventually suicide.

A cry for help ignored by a corrupt justice system,
a system that will only be overcome by making a stand.

On 16 December 2012 in South Delhi, Jyoti Singh was beaten and gang raped in a private bus. She died from her injuries thirteen days later while undergoing emergency treatment in Singapore. The incident generated widespread national and international coverage and was widely condemned, both in India and abroad.

Sohni Mahiwal

A folk love story of Punjab

Between the hidden valleys of the Himalayas
she's in an endless flow- gushing, swishing;
listen to the words of her forbidden love song.

He awaits his loved one. He is the cracked,
dried out earth; his thirst unbearable,
intolerable under the heat of a tropical sun.

She runs into him, screened off from bright
moonlight, she splashes cool sprays of love,
under a web of branches of an old *boor* tree.

Here they merged into one, their love aroused,
integrated, combined making soft muddy soil,
to a perfection. Together they craft rich clay.

Later found by a *kumhar* who moulds, shapes
with his skilful hands into a *ghara*, then fires
it in white heat, hotter than a flying spark.

She is forced to die, fade away, evaporate.
They dissolve into one another; she knows
he will hold her and in the river she will hold him.

boor tree – Indian tree (Punjabi)
kumhar – potter (Punjabi)
ghara – clay pitcher/round jug (Punjabi)

Mistletoe

He kisses her beneath the mistletoe;
how everything now feels so vividly new,
cool winter warmers, pearls of promise, glow.

Energy, affection in frosty snow,
she's excited, amazed, dazed; it's untrue,
he kisses her beneath the mistletoe.

Signifies wholesome life with ample flow,
a desire to dream and embrace love through
cool winter warmers, pearls of promise, glow.

A pure sacred cure, the richness laid low;
she's engraved on his soul like a tattoo,
he kisses her beneath the mistletoe.

Green garlands and translucent berries grow;
crowned queen of hearts in icy diamond dew,
cool winter warmers, pearls of promise, glow.

Adorned with joy, a double ribbon bow,
a magical time, love's moments are few,
he kisses her beneath the mistletoe;
cool winter warmers, pearls of promise, glow.

Silences

My silences have a voice,
come listen to them.
Welcome them in your heart,
watch them blossom.
They're restless to speak,
bottled-up, begging to express.

I utter words in shocking
hushes and shushes,
like the Emperor Aurangzeb's
fatwah; a funeral of all musical art.
Silences, the words of my song,
hum them, sing-along with me.

The rivers flow silently now,
where the flowering moonlight
spreads its love into the darkness.
Crowds of silences are hidden here;
even the raindrops have no speech
as they plunge to their deaths.

There's a silent smoke rising
in my intense heart.
Silences are in the skies;
a spirit that drifts voiceless.
My desires, thoughts vibrate,
still and coloured in emotions.

Exasperated: I write words louder
and quench this muted thirst.

A Sonnet Unheard

Introduction to a noisy world - inspired by hearing aids.

Beneath - scrunching gravel and rocks,
dribbling drips of water tinkle,
the annoying ticking of the clock,
disturbing crisp packets crinkle.

Garden birds sing jubilant songs,
falling raindrops tap-dance pitter,
whispering breeze gossiping strong,
autumn leaves crunch blankets of litter.

Our tiptoes as we creep indoors,
my heart's rhythmic pumping beat,
footsteps clobber on creaky floors,
I hear with aids, murmurs discreet.

Your speech like jewels, sound travels quick,
my fingers type words, click, tick, click.

Kiss

A simple sensuous kiss that touches deep,
I soak in the rains of love - taking me away,
your gentle presence, wakens me from sleep.

You keep my eyes alight; I do not weep.
Your soft lips caress mine, I smile all day,
a simple sensuous kiss that touches deep.

Exhilarating clasp; secrets I'll keep.
Breaking waves as refreshing as sea spray,
your gentle presence, wakens me from sleep.

You make me feel so precious never cheap,
I am eternally yours; I won't betray
a simple sensuous kiss that touches deep.

Your touch is soothing as you softly sweep
me up with a passionate lift. I break away,
your gentle presence wakens me from sleep.

You make my heartbeat pound, dance and leap.
Colour me with memories that surely stay.
A simple sensuous kiss that touches deep,
your gentle presence wakens me from sleep.

Sifting

He watches as the sandy grass stalks beckon,
wild beauty of the dunes, blooms of tiny riches.

He watches them in a labyrinth of captivating colours;
the flowers flourish in the rigid hills and ditches.

He watches the spikes of bottle blue, blood rose,
plum orchids, gorse like tiny lemons warm and sleek.

He watches the olive sea holly, velvet soft and spiky,
in the sand dunes where rabbits play hide and seek.

He watches her as visible as the falling rain,
as she dances bare foot in the slouching sun.

He watches her as she twirls round and round,
her fuchsia dress flares, she seeks joy and fun.

He watches her delicate footprints upon the beach
like memories of a dream – enigmatic and hazy.

He watches as she gives him a secret delight,
drawn to her in an ambiguity – curious and crazy.

He watches the waves crash over the sand blanket,
washing up shells, pebbles, seaweed as the moon rises.

He watches her as she writes his name with driftwood
upon the soft glittering shoreline...

Adder on The Chase

Veiled by shrubs
camouflaged,
she slithers outside
for a bite to eat.
Her scaled khaki
black zigzagged
coat shimmers
in the light like a
dropped necklace.
She's an army
Sergeant Major;
startling serpent,
rarely spotted.
She sits calmly
bathing in the
warmth of the sun
among the green -
she's fully alert.
Like a film star
she is captured
on photographs,
she strikes a pose
yet disappears as
quick as a spark.
Venom protected,
not as deadly as
the Indian Nāgin.
Her silent hush
signals danger.
Watch where you
tread for snakes
in the grass,
keep dogs on leads -
for this cold blooded
reptile could take
you by surprise.
The excitement,
the apprehension
the fear she brings
is simply mysterioussssss.

Nāgin - a female snake of the cobra family.

Bluebell Wood, Baggeridge

We walk along newly ploughed
earth; softened turf like sifted dust,
into open space and pretty woods.

In the distance- saffron sunshine
fields of rapeseed dazzle the eyes,
like an army of luminous pollen.

The gentle enticing, sweet scent
of wild bluebells - tantalizes;
grips, stimulates our senses.

Amethyst embedded ground,
an intense blue-violet carpet,
bursting with life as we walk.

Us girls fascinated by flowers,
chasing brimstone butterflies;
blowing on dandelion clocks.

The boys scamper, dash in and out,
climbing trees, daring each other
to do foolish and risky tricks.

A captivating haze of excitement,
an escape into a timeless world
of winding paths and discovery.

Millions

Definitions of colour, the beauty of intangible dreams,
beliefs, feelings, memories fill the mind in millions.

Walking from the ordinary world into the marvel,
footsteps carry me down a path of desire in millions.

Every breath I take is a drop of love that is energizing,
this heart pounds, I feel my beating heart in millions.

Daisies, blades of grass, the pebbles under my feet,
overwhelmed; the cool drops of rain falling in millions.

Enchantment, the air is caressed with tiny dancing fairies,
born as the wind blows the dandelion seeds in millions.

Birds and insects weave through the leaves and trees,
in all shapes and sizes, all creations of life in millions.

Gazing into the ink-dark sky, I see shining silver glitter,
like scented petals delicately falling off blossom in millions.

People follow another, sheep searching for something lost,
I wish to awaken in this world, shine, be one in millions.

Mine

I have a dream; please don't influence it,
It belongs to me.
I have a delicate heart; please don't break it,
It belongs to me.
I have peace of mind; please don't disturb it,
It belongs to me.
I have to follow a path; please don't obstruct it,
It belongs to me.
I have an amazing life; please let me live it,
It belongs to me.
I have a choice; please don't choose for me,
It belongs to me.
I have freedom; please don't capture me,
It belongs to me.
I have incredible feelings; please don't hurt me,
They belong to me.
I have a lot of love; please don't hate me,
Love is mine to share.
I'm on my material journey; don't follow me
It won't be fair.
So…I have a dream; it's my dream to be free.

Take Off

I dream of exploring all possibilities.
I refuse to be a hush-hush happy frog
in a well-maintained comfort zone.
I feel a need to leap, jump and take off,
run risks and grab opportunities.

I want to take off, not just among
my thoughts and emotions.
I take off my old skin, strip it off
like a snake and leave it far behind.
I show off my new dress. I'm in focus.

I take off along runways in flight -
across the waters to exotic lands,
seasoned in spice, heated sun's rays -
allowing me to take off layers of clothing
right down to my skin. I am a bronze topaz.

I lie on my sun bed, staring upwards,
I am hypnotized by the crystal blueness
of God's eyes - an ocean of creation.
I watch ducks take off, fly and glide,
afloat beneath the deep blue sky.

~

I begin to take off the sheets of stress,
submerging into life worth every second
where there are no rehearsals. I forget my life
as it was and I venture into adventure.
I take off upwards in success and contentment.

I refuse to fall until my last breath, no matter
how many times I fail. I will have no regrets
when I lie in my last peaceful sleep. I am ashes.
I take nothing. I will rise again in another form
like the phoenix, I take off in a new direction.

Whisky

Across the water on a boat,
into the hilly woodlands
with amazing bats and colourful dragonflies;
here the rain comes with no warning.
A couple sit and enjoy the view
from the top of the hill.
After some effort – climbing –
he brings out from his rucksack
a miniature bottle of whisky.
He carefully pours it into a plastic cup,
stands up to nature and gestures with a smile:
"Cheers to this wonderful world!"
then drinks it very slowly.
He offers his wife water and chocolate,
while discussing
an easier route
down the hill.

God Sent

For my husband

Untangled, unknotted; you changed my life into a magical experience.
I want to thank you for coming into my life; you transformed me.

People pitied me, forcing me to believe in something I did not want:
A nothing; a disappointment; a dependent, but you transformed me.

Without you, I was insignificant, just existing and didn't deserve life.
You made this girl into everything, extraordinary, you transformed me.

My dream was to be unique and free. I told myself, "I want to live."
A longing desire to be loved and to give love; yes, you transformed me.

I could not see you; my future had been painted black, by others,
"Who wants a woman like you?" Force-fed; but you transformed me.

Like a princess in a fairytale, I waited for you to sweep me off my feet.
'Be his wife in an ordinary world like this? Absurd?' You transformed me.

You knew I didn't believe in myself, except my prayers were answered.
Now life is just a perfect gift to share. God sent, you transformed me.

Connections

For a Special Soul

I have lived my life like every other person; a naïve angel.
Something I do not understand, our soul connections.

Caught in a special existence; something I can't make out,
a deep essence; searching reasons for our soul connections.

Life connects and realigns, attracting significant souls to me,
yet my life situation will never allow for our soul connections.

Why is it when I see you I sense a power of aged affection?
Time after time we meet not knowing our soul connections.

That instance, the moment we met, our eyes knew something,
tried to analyse and unlock the codes to our soul connections.

I am drawn to you, as though I am already yours somehow,
in a strange but mutual way, we feel our soul connections.

Slowly as time passes, I begin to recognise a familiar link,
enclosed eternal friendship, it's all in our soul connections.

Broken Recovery

For a Surviving Friend

Out of strangers they became friends,
from a great friendship into lovers.
They chose each other; they chose their future,
bound by love, trust, commitment.

She married the one in her fate,
but he had more on his mind.
Days to months; seasons to years,
examined, abandoned, wasted, fooled.

Her reasons turn to madness,
her soul was bankrupt and she broke;
holding on to words as tears gushed,
as if she lay beneath a used spell,
slow suffocation, absence of love.

Reasons flood,
      the earth shreds
           under her feet,
drained she sinks
      into quicksand.
Her pain
      accelerates beyond
          into ever-
              winding thoughts.

Fearful demands,
      she begs to wake up into heavenly bliss.

"Grant me power, present me strength,
give me freedom to love myself;
not only to restore love for others.

When I know I have lost my path,
give me someone who understands;
a patient angel on my shoulder,
a powerful force to guide me back.
I fly with broken wings, I recover."

Shadow

Even through the darkness of night, you lead.
I am with you at every step; I'm your shadow.

Balance your life upon me like a bird on a wire,
I will guide you, protect you, I'm your shadow.

I'll dare you to dream, dare you to play, I care,
sometimes you'll lose me but I'm your shadow.

Don't run after me, let me chase you effortlessly,
I'll make you climb to the top, I'm your shadow.

I beg of you, never drown yourself in grief or pain,
don't be misled, I will hang about, I'm your shadow.

I'll breathe with you, live with you and sleep with you,
life partners until death separates us, I'm your shadow.

Stolen

For Shah Rukh Khan in response to a poem by Aditya Chopra recited by Khan in the Bollywood movie 'Jab Tak Hai Jaan'.

The love in his smile;
the laughter in his eyes;
the sweet forwardness of his lips;
the waves of understanding
unfurled in his voice.
I will never forget him,
until my last breath;
as long as he lives,
as long as I live.

The pleasures I have for small
things without reasons;
I am filled with little, childish mischief.
I dance freely in the rain of his dreams,
with my radiant smile beaming,
I am perfect in his eyes, in his world;
the secret voices I hold within,
he loves them all...
as long as he lives,
as long as I live.

Our true promises;
our burning dreams;
our restless wishes;
our stolen hours together,
we cherish them all,
as long as he lives,
as long as I live.

If he takes his hand away,
and he turns his shadow away from mine;
if he never glances this way again,
I will still forgive him,
until my last breath;
I'll never forget him,
as long as I live.

ACKNOWLEDGEMENTS

Some of these poems have been published in the magazines *Cannon's Mouth* and *Faith Initiative*.

Some have been published in the following anthologies: *We're All In This Together*, 2011, *The Poetry of Shropshire*, 2013, and *The Poetry of Staffordshire*, 2015, all from Offa's Press and the *Blakenhall Writers' Anthology*, 2016.

An Interpretation of Wolverhampton won 3rd prize in the Wolverhampton Archives Poetry Competition, 2011. Some poems were self-published in a booklet *Rag Doll*, 2014.

Mine was published on the Wolverhampton Libraries' website and *Brown Girl in the Rain* and *Sohni Mahiwal* were published on the *Brown Girl* magazine website: www.browngirlmagazine.com.